The
Pocket Book
Of
Paranormal Trivia

How much do YOU know?

Emily A. Georges

Dedications

First and foremost, I would like to dedicate this book to my grandmother, May Nickerson Wallace. I love you and miss you terribly.

To my cousin and published author, Jonathan Knudsen who has been a tremendous inspiration and to my family and friends, simply thank you for believing in me.

Last and most importantly, to my husband Pete who has ALWAYS supported me in my endeavors, I love you very much, honey.

Table of Contents

Introduction

I have been hypnotized by the paranormal's appeal since I was very young. My own personal library of books, cards, games, movies and other exciting paraphernalia is rather extensive in itself. Please know I do not claim to be an expert in any field of paranormal happenings, but I have intensively researched each of the topics I discuss to be sure the answers to all questions laid out in this pocket guide are accurate to the best of my knowledge.

So, chances are good if you are reading this right now you are already familiar with or possibly have an interest in the paranormal (something beyond the range of normal experience or scientific explanation). Well, I do too as I stated previously since I wrote this book of trivia! You will come to see it contains several questions and answers based on a variety of paranormal topics that are entertaining, informational, and even historic in some cases. The questions range in difficulty. Some are very easy while others are a bit challenging even to the occult buff. You will be asked for the definition of a word or for an answer to a question in some cases while offered multiple choice or true or false in others.

This was written solely for your enjoyment. Test yours and other people's paranormal knowledge. You may be surprised what you find out! Memorize it to wow your friends and family members. Strike up a conversation with it. Or, just use it for your own party trivia. It will surely peak interest and get people engaged. So, what are you waiting for? Turn the page and see how much you already know!

Witchcraft

WITCHCRAFT; "THE POWER OR PRACTICE OF A WITCH"

Question: What is the definition of a witch?

Answer: *A person believed to have magic power*

HISTORIC

Question: Where in the United States of America were the witch trials of 1692 held (city, state)?

Answer: *Salem, Massachusetts*

Question: How many people "accused" of witchcraft in Salem, Mass. In 1692 were put to death?

    a) 4

    b) 20

    c) 51

Answer: *b) 20*

Question: How were the 20 individuals in Salem, Mass. put to death?

Answer: *19 were hanged, and 1 was pressed to death*

Question: Billie Burke played which witch in the 1939 movie "The Wizard of Oz"?

Answer: *Glinda*

Question: Who played Endora on the popular 1960's television series "Bewitched"?

Answer: *Agnes Moorehead*

Question: The European witch-hunts lasted from approximately 1450-1750.

TRUE or FALSE

Answer: *True*

Question: All individuals found guilty of being witches during the time span of 1450-1750 were burned to death.

TRUE or FALSE

Answer: *False. Approximately half of those found guilty were indeed burned to death but also hanged. The others were sentenced short of death.*

Question: The term gendercide has been used in association with the European witch-hunts due to the fact so many women (more so than men) were mass murdered.

TRUE or FALSE

Answer: *True*

Question: What is Necromancy?

Answer: *Is a form of divination in which the practitioner seeks to summon "operative spirits" or "spirits of divination", for multiple reasons, from spiritual protection to wisdom*

CURRENT DAY

Question: Do real witches exist?

Answer: *Yes*

Question: Witches practice witchcraft to help better the world and mankind.

                TRUE or FALSE

Answer: *True*

Question: Who is Laurie Cabot?

        a) "Official Witch of Salem"

        b) A fictional character in a story about a witch

        c) One of the accused/murdered individuals in the Salem witch trials

        d) None of the above

Answer: *a) "Official Witch of Salem"*

Question: Name at least one of the organizations Laurie Cabot founded.

Answer: *WLPA (Witches' League for Public Awareness)*
PWP (Project Witches Protection)

Question: What is a coven?

Answer: *An assembly of witches with no more than 13 members*

Question: The Book of Shadows strictly contains spells.

TRUE or FALSE

Answer: *False. It could contain magical practices, ethics and philosophy of the religion. Or, it is simply a personal journal or maybe all of these things.*

Question: Is the athame symbolic for the male or female principle?

Answer: *Male*

10

Question: It is important to know what phase the moon is in while practicing spells and witchcraft.

TRUE or FALSE

Answer: *True*

Question: It is not necessary to practice consecration before using tools in the practice of witchcraft.

TRUE or FALSE

Answer: *False*

Question: Current day witches that are men prefer to be called warlocks.

TRUE or FALSE

Answer: *False. Both men and women prefer the term witch.*

Vampirism

Question: What is the definition of a vampire?

Answer: *The conventional definition is a corpse that rises at night to drink the blood of the living, however not all vampires drink blood.*

Question: Folkloric belief in vampires may be due to the people in pre-industrial societies being ignorant of the body's process of decomposition after death, so to rationalize this mystery they created the figure of the vampire.

TRUE or FALSE

Answer: *True*

Question: Who was the historic Romanian individual that Bram Stoker based his 1897 novel "Dracula" on?

Answer: *Prince Vladislav Dracula of Wallachia*

Question: What was Prince Vlad's preferred method of torture and execution during his reign?

Answer: *Impalement of his victims, hence his more commonly known name "Vlad the Impaler"*

Question: Who played the vampire Count Dracula in Hollywood's 1931 movie, "Dracula"?

Answer: *Bela Lugosi*

Question: What is the name of the author who wrote of psychic parasitism in relation to vampirism in her book entitled "Psychic Self-Defense"?

Answer: *Dion Fortune*

Question: Psychic vampires feed off the life force or energy of other living creatures.

TRUE or FALSE

Answer: *True*

13

Question: Who was the sadistic Hungarian Countess (1560-1614) that tortured and murdered young girls?

Answer: *Elizabeth Bathory*

Question: Which of the following statements is true about Bathory?

a) Bathory believed the blood of young girls could help keep her looking young and retain her vitality

b) She had an aunt who was bisexual

c) She married at the age of 15

d) She would let young girls freeze to death as a form of torture

e) All of the above

Answer: *e) All of the above*

Question: Countess Elizabeth Bathory was present to testify at her own trial.

TRUE or FALSE

Answer: *False. She was walled up in a small chamber in her castle unable to be present at her own trial and eventually died there.*

Question: Bathory is said to have allegedly murdered four-hundred girls and young women.

TRUE or FALSE

Answer: *False. She is said to have murdered over six-hundred.*

Question: Who created Buffy the Vampire Slayer and Angel television series?

Answer: *Joss Whedon*

Question: Sirens are usually portrayed as half bird and half woman.

TRUE or FALSE

Answer: *True*

Question: The term "siren song" refers to an appeal that is hard to resist and, if heeded, will lead to a good result.

TRUE or FALSE

Answer: *False. The end result is always bad. Sirens were depicted as trying to get sailors to shipwreck on rocky coasts or even to lull them to sleep so they could climb aboard and murder them.*

Question: Two illnesses that possibly explain the origin of vampires are Renfield's syndrome (traditionally known as clinical vampirism) and Porphyria.

TRUE or FALSE

Answer: *True.*

Question: Which of the following statements is true about Renfield's syndrome?

a) People who suffer from this disease are usually male

b) Starts as a childhood event of blood ingestion or blood injury

c) There is an erotic attraction for ingesting blood in the hopes to become powerful and immortal

d) It eventually progresses to the consumption of the blood of other creatures

e) All of the above

Answer: *e) All of the above*

16

Question: What actor played Peter Vincent (the vampire killer) in the 1985 movie "Fright Night"?

Answer: *Roddy McDowall*

Question: What is a chupacabra (la chupacabra)?

   a)   A relative of the jackrabbit

   b)   A vampire bat

   c)   A "goat sucker"

Answer: *c) "goat sucker", it's a beast reported to be in the habit of attacking and sucking the blood of livestock, mainly goats (literally means "goat sucker" in Spanish)*

Question: Where and when did the first reported attacks occur where eight sheep were discovered dead, each with three puncture wounds in the chest area and completely drained of blood?

Answer: *Puerto Rico, March 1995*

Question: Are there real current day vampires?

Answer: *Yes*

Question: Current day vampires prefer the spelling vampyre.

TRUE or FALSE

Answer: *True.*

Question: Which of the following statements is true about current day vampyres?

a) You would most likely meet a vampire at a club looking for a donor

b) Vampyres are a subculture of the Goth culture (mainly in the U.S. and Germany)

c) Some exchange blood using a canula

d) All of the above

e) None of the above

Answer: *d) All of the above*

Shape-Shifting

"He who fights with monsters might take care lest he thereby become a monster. And if you gaze for long into an abyss, the abyss gazes also into you."

Friedrich Nietzsche
"Beyond Good and Evil", Aphorism 146

Question: What is Lycanthropy?

Answer: The magical ability to assume the form and characteristics of a wolf

Question: What is the definition of a werewolf?

Answer: A person transformed into a wolf in form and appetite, either temporarily or permanently, whether by supernatural influences, by witchcraft, or voluntarily; a lycanthrope

Question: Who played the werewolf in Hollywood's 1941 movie, "The Wolfman"?

Answer: Lon Chaney Jr.

19

Question: Algonquian tribes of the northern United States and Canada believe in a terrifying creature associated with winter and starvation? Pick the name of the creature in the list below.

     a)   Carnivora

     b)   Wendigo

     c)   Godoba

Answer: *b) Wendigo (also Windigo, Weendigo, Windago, Windiga, Witiko, Wihtikow and other variations)*

Question: The Wendigo mainly craves one thing which is what?

Answer: *Human flesh*

Question: There is a disorder called Wendigo Psychosis that involves an intense craving for human flesh and the fear that one will turn into a cannibal.

TRUE or FALSE

Answer: *True*

Question: What is the name of the author who wrote the 1910 story "The Wendigo"?

Answer: *Algernon Blackwood*

Question: Pick the statement that best describes Therianthropy?

    a) The study of wolves

    b) Psychotic illness where patient thinks he/she is invisible

    c) Refers to the metamorphosis of humans into other animals

Answer: *c) Refers to the metamorphosis of humans into other animals (also known as zoanthropy).*

Question: There is a current day subculture that has formed with individuals calling themselves Therianthropes (most claiming to be part animal in spiritual form).

    TRUE or FALSE

Answer: *True*

Question: Which of the following would not be considered a Therianthrope?

a)   Werewolf

b)   Werecat

c)   Weredog

d)   None of the above

Answer: *d) None of the above*

Question: What is the term for individuals that feel they have not one, but a combination of different theriotypes or weresides?

Answer: *Polywere*

Question: What actor starred as John Kanin in the short lived CBS television series "Wolf Lake"?

Answer: *Lou Diamond Phillips*

Question: In some Native American legends, a person with the supernatural ability to turn into any animal he or she desires is called what?

Answer: *Skin-Walker*

Question: The yee naaldlooshii (meaning literally "with it, he goes on all fours") is a belief relating to which tribe?

   a) Mohawk

   b) Hopi

   c) Navajo

Answer: *c) Navajo*

Question: Which of the following statements is not true of the yee naaldlooshii?

   a) Skinwalkers have the ability to steal the "skin" or body of a person

   b) They are most frequently seen as a coyote, wolf, owl, fox, or crow

   c) Only men can become these skinwalkers

   d) Skinwalkers can have the power to read human thoughts

Answer: *c) Only men can become these skinwalkers*

Question: What is the name of the 1985 movie that tells a tale of a couple cursed by the Bishop causing her to be a hawk by day and him a wolf by night?

Answer: *Ladyhawke*

Question: What is a Nagual or Nahual (both pronounced na'wal)?

Answer: *A human being who has the power to magically turn him or herself into an animal form, most commonly donkey, turkey, and dogs, but also other and more powerful animals.*

Question: The Nagual can use his powers for good or for evil causes according to his personality.

TRUE or FALSE

Answer: *True*

Question: What is Tonalism?

Answer: *It is the belief that a person upon being born requires a close spiritual link to an animal, a link that lasts throughout the lives of both creatures.*

Question: In modern rural Mexico Naguals are believed to only bring good luck among the communities.

TRUE or FALSE

Answer: *False. Naguals are thought to be able to shapeshift into animals at night (normally into an owl, bat or a turkey) and suck blood from innocent victims, steal properties from others, cause disease, etc.*

Question: What are furries?

Answer: *Furries are members of an internet subculture often referred to as "Furry Fandom". They are commonly people who enjoy anthropomorphic animals – animal bearing the attributes of humans. Characters that morph between human and animal form are also considered by some to be part of the genre.*

Question: Furry Lifestylers always take on physical attributes of an animal like hair style (including facial hair), tattoos, articles of clothing (e.g. a tail or ears), or jewelry or even have surgery to affect a physical transformation.

TRUE or FALSE

Answer: *False. This is very rare. They mainly like to role play, and interact online.*

Question: What is an Otherkin?

Answer: *Is a collective term for an assortment of people who have reached the conclusion that they (spiritually, emotionally, mentally and physically) are something other than human.*

Hauntings & Ghosts

HAUNTING; "TO INHABIT, VISIT, OR APPEAR TO IN THE FORM OF A GHOST OR OTHER SUPERNATURAL BEING"

GHOST; "THE SOUL OF A DEAD PERSON, A DISEMBODIED SPIRIT IMAGINED, USUALLY AS A VAGUE, SHADOWY OR EVANESCENT FORM, AS WANDERING AMONG OR HAUNTING LIVING PERSONS"

Question: What is the name of the 1999 film that uses the famous line, "I see dead people."?

Answer: The Sixth Sense

Question: What is an incubus known for doing?

Answer: This evil spirit is said to descend upon women and have sexual intercourse with t hem while they sleep.

Question: What is the counterpart to an incubus?

Answer: Succubus...evil spirit that descends upon men and has sexual intercourse with them while they sleep

Question: What is the name of the 1981 film starring Barbara Hershey that is based on a true story about a woman continually assaulted by an incubus?

Answer: *The Entity*

Question: A Phantom and an Apparition are synonymous with each other?

TRUE or FALSE

Answer: *True*

Question: What is a Poltergeist?

Answer: *Denotes an invisible spirit or ghost that manifests itself by moving and influencing objects, generally in a particular locale such as a house or room or place within a house*

Question: What was the name of the English Rectory back in 1929 that became known as "The Most Haunted House in England"?

Answer: *Borley Rectory*

Question: Who was the paranormal researcher that became famous from investigating the Borley Rectory and writing books about it?

       a) Henry Bull

       b) Reverend Guy Eric Smith

       c) Harry Price

Answer: *c) Harry Price*

Question: What is the name of the best-selling book written by Jay Anson (published in 1977) said to be based on actual paranormal events that led to a series of films released between 1979 and 2005?

Answer: *The Amityville Horror - A True Story*

Question: What is the name of the family that lived in the Dutch Colonial style house in Amityville in 1975 that claims to have been terrorized by paranormal phenomena while in the house?

Answer: *The Lutz family (George, Kathleen and their three children)*

Question: Craig T. Nelson played Steve Freeling in the movie "Poltergeist" but not in the movie "Poltergeist II".

TRUE or FALSE

Answer: *False. He appeared as Steve Freeling in both movies.*

Question: Which of the following statements is true about the Dock Street Theatre located in Charleston, South Carolina?

a) It is thought to possibly be haunted by actor Junius Brutus Booth (father of John Wilkes)

b) The theatre is the original one built in 1736

c) Only one ghost has been seen there

Answer: *a) Thought to be haunted by Junius Brutus Booth (Recall John Wilkes Booth assassinated President Lincoln)*

Question: There is a female spirit seen in the Dock Street Theatre thought to be a prostitute who died from a "botched abortion" in the 1830's.

TRUE or FALSE

Answer: True

Question: A gentleman ghost at the Battery Carriage House Inn in Charleston has a tendency to visit female guests in the night. If they "object" to his presence, what does he do?

Answer: He leaves their room through a wall.

Question: What is the name of the popular television series with two plumbers owning a company called TAPS on the SciFi Channel?

Answer: Ghost Hunters

Question: Who is Marie Laveau?

Answer: A much sought after Voudou Priestess in New Orleans, Louisiana whose wisdom was known around the country

31

Question: Marie Laveau's ghost is reported to haunt only the Myrtles Plantation searching for her lover.

TRUE or FALSE

Answer: *False. She is said to haunt several Orleans locations, including St. Louis Cemetery No. 1, where her body is buried.*

Question: Which of the following statements is false about a New Orleans woman named Delphine LaLaurie (Madame LaLaurie)?

a) She was an American socialite

b) She was a supposed serial killer

c) She was a benevolent slave owner

d) She performed medical experiments on her slaves

e) None of the above

Answer: *c) She was a benevolent slave owner.*

Question: The day after several mutilated slaves were discovered in her home, Madame LaLaurie did not escape the mob demanding justice.

TRUE or FALSE

Answer: *False. She fled and was never heard from again.*

Question: What is the name of the 2002 movie starring Julianna Margulies where a lifeless and haunted 1962 passenger ship was discovered?

Answer: *Ghost Ship*

Question: Which of the following ships is not considered a Ghost Ship?

a)   The Mary Celeste

b)   The Flying Dutchman

c)   Old Glory

d)   The Queen Mary

Answer: *c) Old Glory*

Question: The Mary Celeste is often described as the model
               ghost ship in the sense that it was discovered
               abandoned without any reasonable explanation
               according to the evidence.

               TRUE or FALSE

Answer: *True*

Ufology

UFOLOGY; "THE STUDY OF UNIDENTIFIED FLYING OBJECTS"

Question: What year did the infamous "UFO Incident" occur in Roswell, New Mexico?

Answer: *1947*

Question: Describe the "UFO Incident" that occurred in Roswell, New Mexico in 1947.

Answer: *It is said that an unidentified flying object crashed during the summer of 1947 just outside of Roswell, NM and its wreckage was retrieved by the military. The military first stated it happened then stated it was something else that was found.*

Question: Instead of retrieving a "flying disc" and alien bodies, what did the Air Force claim was found?

Answer: *Weather balloon*

Question: What was the name of the "secret government program" associated with this supposed weather balloon?

Answer: *Project Mogul*

Question: What is the name of the alien planet four teenage alien-human hybrids from the television series "Roswell" are to return to save their race?

Answer: *Antar*

Question: The 1993 movie "Fire in the Sky" is based on a true story.

TRUE or FALSE

Answer: *True*

Question: What is the name of the individual "Fire in the Sky" is about?

Answer: *Travis Walton*

Question: According to Travis, what happened to him on November 5, 1975?

Answer: *He believes he was abducted by extraterrestrials and taken aboard a UFO. He was released five days later.*

Question: What is a crop circle?

a) Agricultural terminology meaning one true bushel

b) Geometric Shape used in Mathematics

c) Circles of bent down plants that appear mysteriously in fields at night

d) None of the above

Answer: *c) Circles of bent down plants that appear mysteriously in fields at night*

Question: All crop circles are indeed circles.

TRUE or FALSE

Answer: *False. Crop circles can be made up of circles, hemispheres, lines, and many other shapes.*

Question: Where around the world do most crop circles seem to occur?

Answer: *2/3 of all crop circles show up in England.*

Question: Through Ufology, various methods have been created to categorize the sightings of UFOs. Who are the two gentlemen that devised some of the more commonly used systems?

Answer;   *Dr. J. Allen Hynek*
             Jacques Vallee

Question: Sightings of UFOs have been reported in which location/time period?

    a) Egypt around 1450 B.C.

    b) Near Kyoto, Japan in 1235

    c) Nuremberg, Germany, 1561

    d) All of the above

    e) None of the above

Answer: *d) All of the above*

Question: There are multiple theories about the existence of extra-terrestrials. What are the two main theories called?

Answer: *ETH or the Extraterrestrial Hypothesis*
IH or the Interdimensional Hypothesis

Question: What year did the popular television series "The X-Files" starring David Duchovny and Gillian Anderson (Mulder and Scully) first air on the Fox network?

Answer: *1993*

Question: Which of the following projects regarding UFO phenomenon investigation was not carried out by the United States Air Force?

a) Project Grudge

b) Project Air

c) Project Sign

d) Project Blue Book

e) None of the above

Answer: *b) Project Air*

Question: What was the number of years dedicated to the investigation of UFOs by the U.S. Air Force according to the "Condon Report"?

Answer: *22 Years*

Question: The "Flap of 1952" was a huge increase in sightings peaking in July with massive sightings both visual and on radar over Washington, D.C.

TRUE or FALSE

Answer: *True*

Question: What was the date the U.S. Air Force officially closed the door on Project Blue Book?

Answer: *January 30, 1970*

Question: A new theory by UFO investigators states that the Earth's core generates electricity which may emerge in certain "hot spots" on the surface of the planet. If you map out Lay Lines in grid formation around the earth, wherever these Lay Lines cross a "hot spot" is known as what?

Answer: *Vortexes*

Question: Which of the following statements is a defining characteristic of a vortex?

a) The place is sacred or hallowed and frequently marked with ancient monuments

b) There is an energy field in that area that differs from the surrounding countryside

c) There is a long term and ongoing history of UFO sightings or other anomalous experiences

d) There is always a military presence nearby

e) All of the above

Answer: *e) All of the above*

Question: Name one of three UFO hot spots currently being investigated as vortexes.

Answer: *Hudson River Valley*
Stonehenge
Sedona, Arizona

Question: What is the name of the 1996 film that portrays spaceships hovering over several major cities all over Earth in early July?

Answer: *Independence Day*

Obscure Religions

"Just as a candle cannot burn without fire, men cannot live without a spiritual life."

Buddha

Question: What is Scientology?

Answer: *It is an applied religious philosophy. In itself the word means literally "knowing how to know". It is further defined as the study and handling of the spirit in relationship to itself, universes, and other life.*

Question: Who is the founder of Scientology?

Answer: *L. Ron Hubbard*

Question: Where was L. Ron Hubbard born (city, state)?

Answer: *Tilden, Nebraska*

Question: What is Dianetics?

Answer: *Hubbard describes Dianetics as, "an organized science of thought built on axioms: statements of natural laws on the order of those of the physical sciences". He describes techniques which he suggests can rid individuals of fears and psychosomatic illnesses.*

Question: Vodun (also known as Voodoo, Vodoun, Vodou) is an African word that means what?

Answer: *Spirit*

Question: Vodoun is approximately 1,000 years old, and its roots stem back to Haiti.

TRUE or FALSE

Answer: *False. Vodoun may be more than 6,000 years old, and its roots stem back to Africa.*

Question: Vodoun is a religion of many traditions. There is a word that means "mystery" in the Yoruba language and is a pantheon of spirits called what?

Answer: *Loa*

Question: There are hundreds of minor spirits in Vodoun. Those which originated from Dahomey are called Rada, and those who were added later are often deceased leaders in the new world and are called Petro.

TRUE or FALSE

Answer: *True*

Question: Which answer below reflects the similarity between Roman Catholicism and Vodoun?

    a) Both believe in a supreme being

    b) Both believe in an afterlife

    c) Both believe in the existence of invisible evil spirits or demons

    d) All of the above

    e) None of the above

Answer: *d) All of the above*

Question: What is the title of the 1988 film starring Bill Pullman as an anthropologist who goes to Haiti to retrieve a drug used by black magic practitioners that turns people into zombies?

Answer: *The Serpent and the Rainbow*

Question: Who is the author of "The Satanic Bible"?

Answer: *Anton Szandor LaVey*

Question: Name the four main books of "The Satanic Bible".

Answer: *"The Book of Satan"*
"The Book of Lucifer"
"The Book of Belial"
"The Book of Leviathan"

Question: What year was the Church of Satan formed?

Answer: *1966*

Question: The Church of Satan recognizes the Christian devil as its deity, and worshippers are encouraged to perform literal human and animal sacrifices.

TRUE or FALSE

Answer: *False. The only "God" a Satanist of this church should worship is him or herself, and LaVey does not condone literal sacrifices of humans and animals in his teachings.*

Question: What day is the most important of all satanic holidays for Church of Satan followers?

Answer: *The individual Satanist's Birthday. The holidays of lesser importance are:*

Walpurgisnacht (April 30th)
Halloween (October 31st)
Solstices in June and December
Equinoxes in March and September

Question: Who is the writer and director of the 1968 American horror/thriller film "Rosemary's Baby"?

Answer: *Roman Polanski*

Question: Wiccans have no reverence for the Earth and believe in only one God.

TRUE or FALSE

Answer: *False. Wicca is an Earth-centered religion, so therefore there is much reverence for the Earth. Additionally, Wiccans have great reverence for their God and Goddess.*

Question: The main rule of behavior for Wiccans is the Wiccan Rede which forbids them from harming people, including themselves.

TRUE or FALSE

Answer: *True*

Question: What does the Threefold Law ("Mind the Threefold Law you should, Three times bad and three times good) mean?

Answer: *Simply put all good that a person does to another returns three fold in this life; harm is also returned three fold.*

Question: What are the eight sabbats Wiccans celebrate?

Answer: *Imbolc*
Ostara
Beltane
Litha
Lammas
Mabon
Samhain
Yule

Question: Although a Pentacle/Pentagram is widely used in the Wiccan religion, what was the symbol most often seen in the television series "Charmed"?

Answer: *The trichetra*

Question: Which of the following statements is not true of the Wiccan belief system?

a) Respect for nature

b) Gender equality

c) Supernatural being in the pantheon of deities resembling the Christian Satan

d) Human sexuality is valued

Answer: *c) Supernatural being in the pantheon of deities resembling the Christian Satan*

Question: What is the name of the actress who starred as Sarah Bailey in the 1996 film entitled "The Craft"?

Answer: *Robin Tunney*

Question: What is the translated meaning of Asatru (Norse Heathenism)?

Answer: *"Asatru" is a combination of "Asa" which is the possessive case of the word Aesir(Gods) and "Tru" which means belief or religion.*

Question: Who was the Icelandic poet who promoted government recognition of Asatru as a legitimate religion which was granted in 1972?

Answer: *Gothi Sveinbjorn Beinteinsson*

Question: Asatru is a polytheistic religion (belief in more than one god).

TRUE or FALSE

Answer: *True*

Question: Name the Nine Noble Virtues North American Astruars have created.

Answer: *Courage, Truth, Honor, Fidelity, Discipline, Hospitality, Industriousness, Self-Reliance, and Perseverance*

Question: Those who die in battle will go to Niflhel.

TRUE or FALSE

Answer: *False. Those who die in battle will be carried to Valhalla by the Valkyries.*

Fortune-Telling

Question: Divination is just another word for Fortune-Telling.

TRUE or FALSE

Answer: *True*

Question: What is Tasseography (also known as Tasseomancy or Tassology)?

Answer: *A divination or fortune-telling method that interprets patterns in tea leaves, coffee grounds, or wine sediments*

Question: When reading the cup, the rim represents the future and farther down into the cup represents the present.

TRUE or FALSE

Answer: *False. It is reversed (the rim represents the present and spiraling down is more distant in time).*

Question: Are tea-leaf symbols and symbolism synonymous with Dream Divination symbols and symbolism?

Answer: *No*

Question: What is the "I-Ching" (also known as "Book of Change", "Yijing", or "I Ging")?

Answer: *It is one of the oldest of the Chinese classic texts. The book is a symbol system used to identify order in chance events. The text is a set of predictions represented by a set of 64 abstract line arrangements called hexagrams. Each hexagram represents a description of a state or process.*

Question: How old is the "I-Ching"?

Answer: *It is over 3,000 years old making it one of the oldest forms of divination.*

Question: What are the methods for casting the hexagrams?

Answer: *Yarrow stalks or the three coin method*

Question: What is astrology?

Answer: *The art of finding cosmic meaning in the patterns of stars and planets*

Question: Tablets with astrological symbols unearthed at the site of ancient Babylon date back to what time period?

Answer: *3,000 B.C*

Question: What is the Zodiac?

Answer: *A belt-shaped region in the heavens on either side to the ecliptic; divided into 12 constellations or signs for astrological purposes*

Question: What are the 12 Zodiac signs?

Answer:
Aquarius
Pisces
Aries
Taurus
Gemini
Cancer
Leo
Virgo
Libra
Scorpio
Sagittarius
Capricorn

Question: If an individual is born May 9th what is his/her Zodiac sign?

a) Capricorn

b) Pisces

c) Gemini

d) None of the above

Answer: *d) None of the above, he/she would be a Taurus*

55

Question: What is the symbol for Aries?

    a) The Scales

    b) The Bull

    c) The Ram

    d) None of the above

Answer: *c) The Ram*

Question: According to the Chinese system of Astrology, the year of birth indicates a certain phase or aspect of a sixty-year cycle of time. Three systems are used for counting and classifying the years. Name the three systems.

Answer: *The ten Heavenly Stems, the twelve Earthly Branches, and the twelve Animals*

Question: What are the 12 Chinese Zodiac signs (animals)?

Answer: *Ox*
                Rat
                Tiger
                Monkey
                Dog
                Dragon
                Boar/Pig
                Snake
                Rabbit/Hare
                Horse
                Rooster/Cock
                Sheep

Question: What are the 5 Chinese elements?

Answer: *Wood*
             Metal
             Fire
             Water
             Earth

Question: What is Feng Shui?

Answer: *One well known definition is the "Ancient Chinese Art of Placement" or more simply Feng Shui aims to increase harmony in your environment (home, workplace, etc.).*

Question: What are the meanings of the words "Feng Shui"?

Answer: *Feng means "wind"*
             Shui means "water"

Question: Dragon Door Feng Shui may be the easiest and most practical method of Feng Shui to use.

TRUE or FALSE

Answer: *True*

Question: What is qi (pronounced "chee")?

Answer: *It is best translated as life energy, vitality, cosmic breath, or the invisible life force.*

Question: Name the Nine Celestial Cures of Feng Shui.

Answer: *1 Reflectors and Lights – mirrors, chandeliers, shiny ribbons, crystals*
2 Goldfish
3 Household Pets
4 Harmonious Sounds – tinkling bells, wind chimes, birdsong, humming insects, whispering wind in bamboo, raindrops and running water
5 Color
6 Plants and Flowers – natural and silk
7 Moving Items – fountains, wind vanes, windmills, rotary doors, rotary fans, grandfather clocks, flag bunting, mobiles, whirligigs, moving lights
8 Heavy Objects – statues, stones
9 Musical Instruments – flutes, fans

Question: What is Cartomancy?

Answer: *The art of telling fortunes with cards*

Question: What are Tarot cards?

Answer: *Any of a set of usually 78 playing cards including 22 cards (Major Arcana) depicting vices, virtues, and elemental forces, used in fortune-telling*

Question: The Rider-Waite Tarot style Tarot deck is the most common set of Tarot cards used by beginners.

TRUE or FALSE

Answer: *True*

Question: What are the four suits of the Minor Arcana in a Tarot deck?

Answer: *Wands*
Swords
Cups
Pentacles

Question: The Court cards almost always indicate people.

TRUE or FALSE

Answer: *True*

Question: The Devil card (XV) literally represents Satan in a reading.

TRUE or FALSE

Answer: *False. This card represents things we are taught to view as evil or shameful; examples are earthly materialism, sexual desire, valuables, food, drugs, lack of control, excess, obsession and raw ambition.*

Question: What is Numerology?

Answer: *The study of numbers and their symbolic significance*

Question: Which one of the following is believed to have developed their own system of numerology in order to understand nature?

    a) Mayans

    b) Tibetans

    c) Celts

    d) All of the above

Answer: *d) All of the above*

Question: Odd numbers such as one, three, five, seven, and nine are believed to possess a feminine energy.

TRUE or FALSE

Answer: *False. Odd numbers are believed to possess a masculine energy.*

Question: A birth date number and its shadow number always add up to what number?

Answer: *Nine*

Question: In Numerology your personal name has a number with importance and meaning.

TRUE or FALSE

Answer: True

Question: What are the three master numbers not usually reduced to a single digit?

Answer: Eleven
Twenty-two
Thirty-three

Question: What is Pessomancy (also known as Psephology or Psephomancy)?

Answer: Divination by pebbles, stones, rocks or even beans marked with symbols and colors relating to issues such as health, communications, success, and travel

Question: The stones in Pessomancy are always thrown out after shuffling them in a bag.

TRUE or FALSE

Answer: *False. They are either thrown out after shuffling them in a bag or drawn out at random.*

Question: What is Scrying?

Answer: *Scrying is a magic practice that involves seeing things psychically in a medium, usually for purposes of obtaining spiritual visions and for purposes of divination or fortune-telling.*

Question: What objects are commonly used for Scrying?

Answer: *The items most commonly used are reflective, translucent, or luminescent substances such as crystals, stones, glass, mirrors, water, fire, or smoke.*

Question: Crystal Ball gazing is the most popular and therefore most recognized form of Scrying.

TRUE or FALSE

Answer: *True*

Question: A crystal ball has magical powers or supernatural qualities that enable it to foresee the future.

TRUE or FALSE

Answer: *False. It is the clearness of the crystal that gives it extraordinary scrying qualities to assist the seer in forming images in his or her "mind's eye" and not in the ball itself.*

Question: What is Carromancy (also known as Ceromancy)?

Answer: *Is a form of divination using wax*

Question: Wax divination is practiced by heating wax until molten and then pouring it directly into cold water as well as just simply studying the flame of a burning candle to predict the future.

TRUE or FALSE

Answer: *True*

Question: What is an Ouija board?

Answer: *An Ouija board (pronounced "weejah" and also known as a spirit board or talking board) is any flat board with letters, numbers, and other symbols, used to communicate with spirits. It uses a planchette or movable indicator to indicate the message by spelling it out on the board during a séance.*

Question: Where was the first historical mention of something resembling an Ouija board around in 1200 B.C.?

Answer: *China.*

Question: Which of the following individuals frowned upon the use of the Ouija board?

a) Frater Achad (Charles Stansfeld Jones)

b) Jane Wolf

c) Aleister Crowley

d) Edgar Cayce

Answer: *d) Edgar Cayce*

Paranormal Abilities

"There was something awesome in the thought of the solitary mortal standing by the open window and summoning in from the gloom outside the spirits of the nether world."

Sir Arthur Conan Doyle

Question: Is there a difference between Telekinesis and Psychokinesis?

Answer: *No*

Question: What is Telekinesis and/or Psychokinesis?

Answer: *The power to move something by thinking about it without the application of physical force*

Question: This ability is frequently defined, close to intuition, as psychical manifestations that cannot be perceived in any other manner.

    a) Clairaudience

    b) Clairsentience

    c) Clairvoyance

Answer: *b) Clairsentience*

Question: What is the ability associated with seeing the future and not visions in a distant place?

Answer: *Clairvoyance*

Question: What is the ability to describe a scene that is taking place miles away?

Answer: *Remote Viewing*

Question: What does ESP stand for?

Answer: *Extra Sensory Perception*

Question: What is a medium?

Answer: *Person thought to have the power to communicate with the spirits of the dead or with agents of another world or dimension*

Question: Who is the internationally known psychic medium, author, and lecturer who had a television series entitled, "Crossing Over"?

Answer: *John Edward*

Question: How does a medium communicate with the spirits of the dead?

Answer: *Channeling; the practice of professedly entering a meditative or trancelike state in order to convey messages from a spiritual guide*

Question: What was the name of the medium who claimed to "channel" a personality by the name of Seth?

Answer: *Jane Roberts*

Question: The messages (mostly monologues on a variety of topics), channeled by Seth through Jane Roberts, are collectively known as what?

Answer: *The Seth Material*

Question: What is the name of the actress that stars in the NBC television series "Medium"?

Answer: *Patricia Arquette*

Question: Edgar Cayce has been called the "sleeping prophet", the "father of holistic medicine", and the most documented psychic of the 20th century. Cayce gave psychic "readings" to thousands of seekers while in an unconscious state, diagnosing illnesses and revealing lives lived in the past and prophecies yet to come.

TRUE or FALSE

Answer: *True*

Question: What is Automatic Writing?

Answer: *The process or production of writing material, while usually in a trance-like state, that does not come from the conscious thoughts of the writer.*

Question: Automatic writing is great for self discovery or starting a writing project.

TRUE or FALSE

Answer: *True*

Question: What is Astral Projection or Astral Travel?

Answer: *Refers to episodes of out-of-body experiences perceived as unfolding in environments other than the physical world, by an astral counterpart of the physical body that separates from it and travels to one or more astral planes*

Question: Which individual popularized the term "OBE" (out-of-body experience)?

a) Sylvan Muldoon

b) Robert Monroe

c) Robert Bruce

Answer: *b) Robert Monroe*

Question: During astral projection, you remain attached to your body through a silver "umbilical like" cord.

TRUE or FALSE

Answer: *True*

Question: What is creative visualization?

Answer: *It is the technique of using your imagination to create what you want in your life.*

Question: What is the name of the author who wrote the book entitled "Creative Visualization"?

Answer: *Shakti Gawain*

Question: There are four basic steps for effective creative visualization. Which of the following statements is not one of the steps?

      a) Set Your Goal

      b) You <u>must</u> have a mental image in your mind

      c) Focus on it often

      d) Give it positive energy

Answer: *b) You must have a mental image in your mind*
The answer is only partially correct to the second step of effective creative visualization. Some people cannot truly see images in their minds, so a clear idea is effective enough.

Question: Gawain believes there are three levels in life; beingness, doingness, and havingness. These three states are not in conflict with each other and exist simultaneously.

TRUE or FALSE

Answer: *True*

Question: Gawain also believes there are three elements within us that will determine how successful creative visualization will work for us. The elements are Desire, Belief, and Acceptance. The sum total of these three is called what?

Answer: *Intention*

Question: Creative visualization is not a tool for creating and maintaining good health.

TRUE or FALSE

Answer: *False*

Question: What is an aura?

Answer: *A field of subtle, luminous radiation surrounding a person or object, and each color of the aura has a precise meaning, indicating a precise emotional state*

Question: Colors and intensity of the aura, especially around and above the head have very special meanings. It reflects the true nature and intentions of the individual.

TRUE or FALSE

Answer: *True*

Question: Real colors are surrounded with auras of different colors called auric pairs. Which of the following is an auric pair?

    a) Yellow gives violet aura, violet gives yellow aura

    b) Green gives blue aura, blue gives green aura

    c) Red gives orange aura, orange gives red aura

    d) Purple gives pink aura, pink gives purple aura

Answer: *a) Yellow gives violet aura, violet gives yellow aura*

Question: A red aura indicates materialistic thoughts and thoughts about the physical body. A predominantly red aura indicates a materialistically oriented person.

TRUE or FALSE

Answer: *True*

Question: The character Sam Winchester on the popular television series "Supernatural" obtained his special powers from what?

Answer: *Ingesting demon blood as an infant*

Bibliography

Barrett, Hilary. *I Ching with Clarity*. 4 Mar. 2009 <http://www.onlineclarity.co.uk/>.

Benecke, Mark. "Vampires Among Us". *Benecke.com*. Ed. Mark Benecke. 27 June 2008. 23 Mar. 2009 <http://www.wiki.benecke.com/index.php?title=Vampires_among_us:_Vampire_Subcultures_%26_an_interview_with_a_female_vampire>.

Cabot, Laurie. *LaurieCabot.com*. 5 Feb. 2009 <http://LaurieCabot.com/Official_Witch.html>.

"Chinese Astrology". *Astrology.com*. 1995-2007. Ivillage Inc. 8 Mar. 2009 <http://chinese.astrology.com/default.aspx>.

Dictionary.com. 2009. Dictionary.com, LLC. <http://dictionary.reference.com/browse/...>.

Eason, Cassandra. *The Complete Guide to Psychic Development*. London: Judy Piatkus (Publishers), 1997.

Edward, John. *One Last Time*. New York: The Berkley Publishing Group, Oct. 1999.

Farrell, Patricia. *Numerology*. Rockport: Element Books Inc., 1997.

Gawain, Shakti. *Creative Visualization*. New York: Bantam Doubleday Dell Publishing Group, Oct. 1982.

"Haitian Voodoo". *Travelinghaiti.com*. 2009. 20 Mar. 2009 <http://travelinghaiti.com/haitian_voodoo.asp>.

Hall, Molly. "Ancient Civilizations and Astrology". *About.com*. The New York Times Company. 20 Feb. 2009 <http://astrology. about.com/od/thehistoryofastrology/a/AncientStars.htm>.

"Haunted History: Charleston". *The Cold Spot*. Ed. John H. Witzig. 24 Mar. 2009 <http://www.theflagship.net/coldspot/docs/ hauntedhistory-Charleston.html>.

"Haunted History: New Orleans". *The Cold Spot*. Ed. John H. Witzig. 24 Mar. 2009 <http://www.theflagship.net/coldspot/ docs/hauntedhistory-neworleans.html>.

"History of UFOs". *History.com*. 2006. An Article from *Funk & Wagnalls New Encyclopedia*. World Almanac Education Group, A WRC Media Company. 14 Mar. 2009 <http://www. history.com/content/ufohunters/history-of-ufos>.

Hubbard, L. Ron. *Dianetics, The Modern Science of Mental Health*. Los Angeles: Bridge Publications, Inc., 1992.

Imdb.com. 1990-2009. IMDb.com, Inc. <http://www.imdb.com/ title/>.

Jacobsen, Sharon. "Crystal Ball Gazing". Crystal Ball Gazing. 21 Oct. 2005. *EzineaArticles.com*. 22 Mar. 2009 <http:// ezinearticles.com/?Crystal-Ball-Gazing&id=85421>.

King, Teri. *Love, Sex and Astrology*. New York: HarperPaperbacks, 1994.

Mama Zogbe. "Voodoo, A Brief History of Vodoun." *Mamiwata.com*. Ed. Mama Zogbe. 2008. 20 Mar. 2009 <http://www.mamiwata.com/voodoohistory.html>.

"Project Blue Book". *Ufocasebook.com*. 26 Mar. 2009 *Ufocasebook.com*. 26 Mar. 2009 <http://www.ufocasebook. com/bluebook.html>.

Quotation Search." *Quotationspage.com.* 1994-2007.
QuotationsPage.com and Michael Moncur. 19 Mar. 2009
<http://www.quotationspage.com./search.php3>.

Religioustolerance.org. 1995-2009. Ontario Consultants on
Religious Tolerance. 21 Mar. 2009 <http://www.religious
tolerance.org>.

Summers, Selena. *Feng Shui in 5 Minutes.* Woodbury: Llewellyn
Publications, 2002.

Therianthropes United. *Therianthropes.com.* 26 Mar. 2009
<http://www.therianthropes.com/>.

Thiaboouba. "How to see and read the aura". *Thiaboouba.com.* 26
Mar. 2009 <http://www.thiaboouba.com/see_aura_color.htm>.

Thirteen. "Tarot Card Meanings." *Aeclectic Tarot.* Ed. Solandia.
1996-2007. 12 Mar. 2009 <http://www.aeclectic.net/tarot/learn/
meanings/>.

Ward, Margarete. *Gong Hee Fot Choy.* Berkeley: Celestial Arts,
1982.

"Who Was Elizabeth Bathory?". 12 Mar. 2009 <http://www.
geocites.com./Wellesley/Veranda/7128/>.

Wikipedia.org. 2009. Wikipedia Foundation, Inc.
<http://en.wikipedia.org/wiki/>.

Wilson, Joyce. *The Complete Book of Palmistry.* New York: Bantam
Books with Workman Publishing Company, Inc., 1971.

"Witchcraft Spells". *Witchcraft.com.* 22 Mar. 2009 <http://www.
witchcraft.com.au/witchcraft_spells.html#constructivespells>.